TWO BY TWO

THE STORY OF NOAH'S FAITH

By Marilyn Lashbrook

Illustrated by Stephanie McFetridge Britt

ME TOO!
B O O K S

ROPER PRESS, INC.
DALLAS, TEXAS

Noah's Ark has long been a favorite of young children. In addition to learning about Noah's faith and God's faithfulness, your child will have fun learning animal sounds and rainbow colors. After each question on pages 10-19, stop and allow your child to tell you what each animal says. Page 29 can be used two ways to teach colors. You may point and ask your child to say the color, or you may wish to say the color and ask your child to point to it. Share with your little ones in simple words your own faith in God.

Library of Congress Catalog Card Number: 87-60263
ISBN 0-86606-427-3

Art direction and design by
  Chris Schechner Graphic Design

TWO BY TWO

THE STORY OF NOAH'S FAITH

By Marilyn Lashbrook

Illustrated by Stephanie McFetridge Britt

Taken from Genesis 6 to 8

ME TOO!
BOOKS

Noah was God's friend.
He believed what God said ...
God always tells the truth.

One day, God told Noah
there would be a flood.
"You must build
a great big boat," God said.

Nobody knew what a flood was.

But Noah believed God.

So he gathered enough wood
to build a great big boat.
Tap, tap, tap. Rap, rap, rap.

Noah worked very hard.
He made the boat
just the way God told Him to,
for Noah believed everything God said.

People came to see what Noah was doing.
When they saw the big boat,
they laughed and laughed.
"There is no water here!" they said.
"Where will you float your boat?"

Noah told the people what God said,
but they did not believe.
Noah went back to work.
He knew what God said was true.

One day the boat was finished.
"Now," God said,
"I will bring two of every kind of animal

to ride on the boat with you."
Noah waited for the animals to come.

The frisky puppies came two by two.
What do the puppies say to you? (bow, wow)

The soft furry kittens came two by two.
What do the kittens say to you? (meow)

The waddling ducks came two by two.
What do the ducks say to you? (quack, quack)

The spotted cows came two by two.
What do the cows say to you? (moo)

The curly-tailed pigs came two by two.
What do the pigs say to you? (oink, oink)

The wooly sheep came two by two.
What do the sheep say to you? (baa, baa)

The tiny mice came two by two.
What do the mice say to you? (squeek, squeek)

The great big bears came two by two.
What do the bears say to you? (grrrrrr)

The animals came two by two,
elephants, lions and monkeys, too.
Noah led them all into the boat.

"Bang!" God shut the door.
They were all safe inside.

Drip, drip, drip
the raindrops fell softly.
Splish, splash, splish.
They made puddles on the ground.

The lightning flashed!
The thunder cracked!
Down, down, down
the heavy rain fell.

Noah's boat rocked
a little this way
and a little that way.
It was starting to float.

For forty days and forty nights
it rained, and rained, and rained.
The water rose higher and higher.
And the big boat stayed right on top
with Noah and the animals safe inside.

Then something happened. Noah listened.
He did not hear the rain.

Slowly, very slowly,
the flood waters dried away.

One day, the big boat landed
on the top of a large mountain.

When God said it was time,
Noah let the animals out of the boat.
Two by two they marched
down the mountain
to look for new homes.

I will never again
cover the earth with water," God promised.
"And as a reminder,
I will put a rainbow in the sky."

Can you tell me the colors of the rainbow?
(red, orange, yellow, green, blue, purple)

Noah looked at the beautiful rainbow.
He knew what God promised was true.